Piano · Vocal · Guitar

Disco Lives!

ISBN 0-7935-5058-0

HAL·LEONARD™
CORPORATION
7777 W. BLUEMOUND RD. P.O. BOX 13819 MILWAUKEE, WI 53213

CONTENTS

Disco Lives!

BOOGIE FEVER

Words and Music by FREDERICK PERREN
and KENNETH ST. LEWIS

COPACABANA
(AT THE COPA)

Words by BRUCE SUSSMAN and JACK FELDMAN
Music by BARRY MANILOW

BOOGIE WONDERLAND

Words and Music by JOHN LIND
and ALLEE WILLIS

FUNKYTOWN

Words and Music by
STEVEN GREENBERG

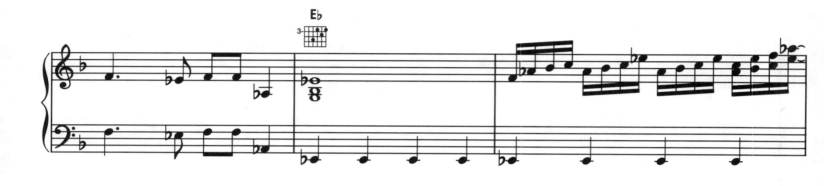

Got - ta move on.___

Got - ta move on.___

no chord

Fm7

Won't you take me to

26

D.S. al Coda

Well,   I

CODA

Got - ta move on.____

Repeat and Fade

Got - ta move on.____   Oo.____

HEAVEN MUST BE MISSING AN ANGEL

Words and Music by FREDERICK PERREN
and KENNETH ST. LEWIS

HEAVEN KNOWS

Words and Music by DONNA SUMMER, GIORGIO MORODER,
PETE BELLOTTE and GREG MATHIESON

Coda

Heav - en knows ___ it's not the way it should be, I just

had to stop, ___ I had to stop pre - tend-ing, so come on now, ___

hear me when I cry. _____

HOT STUFF

Words and Music by PETE BELLOTE,
HAROLD FALTERMEYER and KEITH FORSEY

HOT LINE

Words and Music by FREDERICK PERREN
and KENNETH ST. LEWIS

I JUST WANT TO BE YOUR EVERYTHING

Words and Music by
BARRY GIBB

I WILL SURVIVE

Words and Music by DINO FEKARIS
and FREDDIE PERREN

IF I CAN'T HAVE YOU

Words and Music by BARRY GIBB,
MAURICE GIBB and ROBIN GIBB

IN THE NAVY

Words and Music by JACQUES MORALI,
HENRI BELOLO and VICTOR WILLIS

1. Where can you find pleas - ure, search ___ the world for treas - ure,
2. Where can you learn to fly, play ___ in sports or skin dive,
3. *(See additional lyrics)*

learn sci - ence tech - nol - o - gy? ___
stud - y o - cean - og - ra - phy? ___

Additional Lyrics

3. If you like adventure,
   Don't you wait to enter
   The recruiting office fast.
   Don't you hesitate,
   There is no need to wait;
   They're signing up new seamen fast.
   Maybe you are too young to join up today,
   But don't you worry 'bout a thing,
   For I'm sure there will be always
   The good navy protecting the land and sea.
   To Chorus:

IT ONLY TAKES A MINUTE

Words and Music by DENNIS LAMBERT
and BRIAN POTTER

LAST DANCE

Words and Music by
PAUL JABARA

JIVE TALKIN'
from SATURDAY NIGHT FEVER

Words and Music by BARRY GIBB,
MAURICE GIBB and ROBIN GIBB

Moderately, with a strong beat

LOVE TO LOVE YOU, BABY

Words and Music by DONNA SUMMER,
GIORGIO MORODER and PETER BELLOTTE

LOVE IS THICKER THAN WATER

Words and Music by BARRY GIBB
and ANDY GIBB

MacARTHUR PARK

Words and Music by
JIMMY WEBB

Spring was nev-er wait-ing ___ for us,
I re-call the yel-low cot-ton

girl, it ran ___ one ___ step a-head as we fol-lowed in ___ the
dress foam-ing like a wave on the ground a-round your

84

There will be an-oth-er song_ for me for I will sing_____ it,____

there will be an-oth-er dream for me, some-one will

Mac - Ar-thur's Park is melt-ing   in the dark,   all the sweet green ic-ing

MACHO MAN

Words and Music by JACQUES MORALI, HENRI BELOLO,
VICTOR WILLIS and PETER WHITEHEAD

Additional Lyrics

D.C. Body, it's so hot, my body,
Body, love to pop my body.
Body, love to please my body.
Body, don't you tease my body.
Body, you'll adore my body.
Body, come explore my body.
Body, made by God, my body.
Body, it's so good, my body.

3. Ev'ry man ought to be a macho man.
To live a life of freedom machos make a stand.
Have their own life style and ideals.
Possess the strength and confidence life's a steal.
You can best believe that he's a macho man.
He's a special person in anybody's land.
To Chorus:

MORE THAN A WOMAN

from SATURDAY NIGHT FEVER

Words and Music by BARRY GIBB,
MAURICE GIBB and ROBIN GIBB

Medium Disco beat

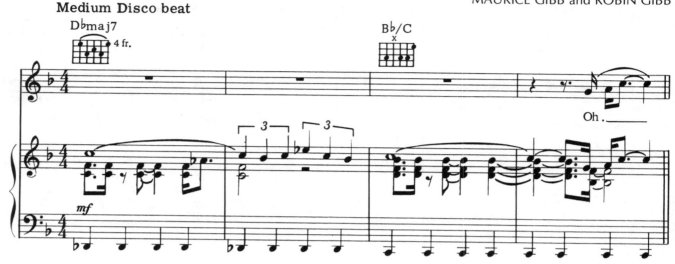

Oh. ____

Girl, I've known you ver - - y well. I've seen you grow - in' ev - 'ry day.__ I nev-
There are sto - ries old__ and true of peo - ple so__ in love__ like you__ and me,__

er real - ly looked__ be - fore,__ but now you take my breath a - way.__
__ and I__ can see__ my - self__ let his - to - ry re - peat it - self.__ Re-

NIGHT FEVER
from SATURDAY NIGHT FEVER

Words and Music by BARRY GIBB,
MAURICE GIBB and ROBIN GIBB

NO MORE TEARS
(ENOUGH IS ENOUGH)

Words and Music by PAUL JABARA
and BRUCE ROBERTS

ENOUGH IS ENOUGH

you've had e-nough don't put up with his stuff, don't you do_____ it.____

If you've had your fill get the check,___ pay the bill,___ you can

NIGHTS ON BROADWAY

Words and Music by BARRY GIBB,
MAURICE GIBB and ROBIN GIBB

ON THE RADIO

Words and Music by GIORGIO MORODER
and DONNA SUMMER

SHADOW DANCING

Words and Music by BARRY GIBB,
ROBIN GIBB, MAURICE GIBB and ANDY GIBB

You got me look-ing at that heav-en in— your eyes. I was
All that I need— is just one mo-ment in— your arms. I was

chas-ing your_ di- rec - tion. I was tell- ing you_ no lies_ and I was
chas-ing your_ af- fec - tion. I was do- ing you_ no harm_ and I was

SHAKE YOUR GROOVE THING

Words and Music by DINO FEKARIS
and FREDDIE PARREN

STAYIN' ALIVE
from SATURDAY NIGHT FEVER

Words and Music by BARRY GIBB,
MAURICE GIBB and ROBIN GIBB

SHAME

from the Original Motion Picture Soundtrack A LOW DOWN DIRTY SHAME

Words and Music by JOHN FITCH
and REUBEN CROSS

Y.M.C.A.

Words and Music by JACQUES MORALI,
HENRI BELOLO and VICTOR WILLIS

1. Young man,   there's no   need to feel down._ I said,
2.,3. *(See additional lyrics)*

Em

young man, pick your-self off the ground. __ I said,

C

young man, 'cause you're in a new town __ there's no

D/F♯   **C/E**   **D**   **C**   **G/B**   **D/A**

need to _____ be _____ un - hap - py.

G

Young man, there's a place you can go, _____ I said,

Repeat ad lib. and Fade

ev - er - y - thing___ for young men to en - joy.___ You can

hang out with all ___ the boys. ___ It's fun to stay at the

Additional Lyrics

2. Young man, are you listening to me?
   I said, young man what do you want to be?
   I said, young man you can make real your dreams
   But you've got to know this one thing.

   No man does it all by himself.
   I said young man put your pride on the shelf.
   And just go there to the Y.M.C.A.
   I'm sure they can help you today.
   To Chorus:

3. Young man, I was once in your shoes
   I said, I was down and out and with the blues.
   I felt no man cared if I were alive.
   I felt the whole world was so jive.

   That's when someone come up to me
   And said, "Young man, take a walk up the street.
   It's a place there called the Y.M.C.A.
   They can start you back on your way."
   To Chorus:

YOU MAKE ME FEEL LIKE DANCING

Words and Music by VINI PONCIA
and LEO SAYER

Moderate Disco beat

You've got a cute way of talk - ing;
Quar - ter to four in the morn - ing,

you got the bet - ter of me.___
I ain't feel - ing tired, no, no, no.___

Just snap your fin - gers and I'm
Just hold me tight and leave on

walk - ing   like a dog   hang-ing on your lead.
the ___ light,   like a   'cause I   don't   wan - na go ___ home.

TRAGEDY

Words and Music by BARRY GIBB,
MAURICE GIBB and ROBIN GIBB

Here I lie in a lost and lone-ly part of town,
Night and day there's a burn-ing down in-side of me.

Trag - e - dy,__ when the feel - ing's gone and you can't go on, it's

trag - e - dy;__ when the morn - ing cries and you don't know why, it's

hard to bear__ with no one to love you you're go - in' no - where.

Trag - e - dy,__ when you lose con - trol and you got no soul, it's

YOU SHOULD BE DANCING

from SATURDAY NIGHT FEVER

Words and Music by BARRY GIBB,
MAURICE GIBB and ROBIN GIBB

YOU SEXY THING

Words and Music by
E. BROWN

I be-lieve in mir-a-cles.___

Where you from, ___ you sex - y thing. ___
(You sex - y thing, you.)

I be-lieve in mir-a-cles____ since you came a-long,___

you sex-y thing. ____

Where did you come from, ba - by? How did you know____ I
Where did you come from, an - gel? How did you know____ I'd

Contemporary Classics

Your favorite songs for piano, voice and guitar.

The Definitive Rock 'n' Roll Collection

A classic collection of the best songs from the early rock 'n' roll years – 1955-1966. 97 songs, including: Barbara Ann • Chantilly Lace • Dream Lover • Duke Of Earl • Earth Angel • Great Balls Of Fire • Louie, Louie • Rock Around The Clock • Ruby Baby • Runaway • (Seven Little Girls) Sitting In The Back Seat • Stay • Surfin' U.S.A. • Wild Thing • Woolly Bully • and more.
00490195 ....$24.95

The Big Book Of Rock

78 of rock's biggest hits, including: Addicted To Love • American Pie • Born To Be Wild • Cold As Ice • Dust In The Wind • Free Bird • Goodbye Yellow Brick Road • Groovin' • Hey Jude • I Love Rock N Roll • Lay Down Sally • Layla • Livin' On A Prayer • Louie Louie • Maggie May • Me And Bobby McGee • Monday, Monday • Owner Of A Lonely Heart • Shout • Walk This Way • We Didn't Start The Fire • You Really Got Me • and more.
00311566...$19.95

Big Book Of Movie And TV Themes

Over 90 familiar themes, including: Alfred Hitchcock Theme • Beauty And The Beast • Candle On The Water • Theme From *E.T.* • Endless Love • Hawaii Five-O • I Love Lucy • Theme From *Jaws* • Jetsons • Major Dad Theme • The Masterpiece • Mickey Mouse March • The Munsters Theme • Theme From *Murder, She Wrote* • Mystery • Somewhere Out There • Unchained Melody • Won't You Be My Neighbor • and more!
00311582 ....$19.95

The Best Rock Songs Ever

70 of the best rock songs from yesterday and today, including: All Day And All Of The Night • All Shook Up • Ballroom Blitz • Bennie And The Jets • Blue Suede Shoes • Born To Be Wild • Boys Are Back In Town • Every Breath You Take • Faith • Free Bird • Hey Jude • I Still Haven't Found What I'm Looking For • Livin' On A Prayer • Lola • Louie Louie • Maggie May • Money • (She's) Some Kind Of Wonderful • Takin' Care Of Business • Walk This Way • We Didn't Start The Fire • We Got The Beat • Wild Thing • more!
00490424 ....$16.95

The Best Of 90s Rock

30 songs, including: Alive • I'd Do Anything For Love (But I Won't Do That) • Livin' On The Edge • Losing My Religion • Two Princes • Walking On Broken Glass • Wind Of Change • and more.
00311668 ....$14.95

35 Classic Hits

35 contemporary favorites, including: Beauty And The Beast • Dust In The Wind • Just The Way You Are • Moon River • The River Of Dreams • Somewhere Out There • Tears In Heaven • When I Fall In Love • A Whole New World (Aladdin's Theme) • and more.
00311654 ....$12.95

55 Contemporary Standards

55 favorites, including: Alfie • Beauty And The Beast • Can't Help Falling In Love • Candle In The Wind • Have I Told You Lately • How Am I Supposed To Live Without You • Memory • The River Of Dreams • Sea Of Love • Tears In Heaven • Up Where We Belong • When I Fall In Love • and more.
00311670 ....$15.95

The New Grammy® Awards Song Of The Year Songbook

Every song named Grammy Awards' "Song Of The Year" from 1958 to 1988. 28 songs, featuring: Volare • Moon River • The Shadow Of Your Smile • Up, Up and Away • Bridge Over Troubled Water • You've Got A Friend • Killing Me Softly With His Song • The Way We Were • You Light Up My Life • Evergreen • Sailing • Bette Davis Eyes • We Are The World • That's What Friends Are For • Somewhere Out There • Don't Worry, Be Happy.
00359932 ....$12.95

Soft Rock – Revised

39 romantic mellow hits, including: Beauty And The Beast • Don't Know Much • Save The Best For Last • Vision Of Love • Just Once • Dust In The Wind • Just The Way You Are • Your Song.
00311596 ....$14.95

37 Super Hits Of The Superstars

37 big hits by today's most popular artists, including Billy Joel, Amy Grant, Elton John, Rod Stewart, Mariah Carey, Wilson Phillips, Paula Abdul and many more. Songs include: Addicted To Love • Baby Baby • Endless Love • Here And Now • Hold On • Lost In Your Eyes • Love Takes Time • Vision Of Love • We Didn't Start The Fire.
00311539 ....$14.95

Prices, contents & availability subject to change without notice.